Contrasts

NOW
& Then

**A Plateau Area Writers
Association Anthology**

Contrasts is an themed anthology publication of the Plateau Area Writers Association of aspiring and accomplished authors concentrated in communities of South King and North Pierce Counties bordering the foothills of the Cascade Mountains in the state of Washington and members from seven other states.

ISBN: 978-0-916262-77-8
ISSN: 2332-0338
Steilacoom, Washington. USA
Trescott Research
Plateau Area Writers Association
Buckley, Washington
Annual (2010-   )

Paul T. Jackson, Editor
Trescott@umich.edu

http://ers.org/   plateauareawrit-ers.org/

ISSN 2332-0338

9 772434 561006

DEDICATION

A special dedication to those who started, worked hard, and grew Plateau Area Writers Association over the 20 years. A few have died, others remain, some in diminished capacity, and others came. In all, they worked together to help each other as writers along the lonesome way, and pre-served a place for new writers to be seen and heard and read.
...Bravo!

The Present Plateau Area Writer's Roster
[First Quarter, from the Dec. 1998 meeting]

Miriam Bowers
Richard Brugger, Newsletter Editor
Louise Deffley
Elaine Estes*
Carol Lynn Harp, *Program Chair for the March Meeting*
Emmy Knemeyer*
Dorothea Kreklow,* *Chair for the March Meeting*
Jeff Opheim*

* deceased

CONTENTS

Foreword:

The Plateau Area Writers Association (PAWA) members have been producing two publications since 2002. These are a Quarterly and a themed Anthology. The latter has had many titles, until 2010 when the work became an annual publication under a series title, *Contrasts.*

1. 2002 Remember
2. 2003 PAWA Full Fiction
3. 2003 We Were Young Once
4. 2004 Winter Stories
5. 2005 Unexpected Heroes
6. 2006 Reigning Cats and Dogs
7. 2006 Celebrations
8. 2007 Fact, Fiction or Farce
9. 2007 Defining Moments
10. 2008 Scary Moments
11. 2008 Potpourri
12. 2009 Sweet Dreams and Nightmares
13. 2009 Stories for Young Readers
14. 2010 Magical Moments; Unexplained Events
15. 2010 CONTRASTS: Apples and Oranges
16. 2011 CONTRASTS: Guilt or Innocence
17. 2012 CONTRASTS: More or Less
18. 2013 CONTRASTS: Coffee or Tea
19. 2014 CONTRASTS: Before and After
20. 2015 CONTRASTS: Here and/or There
21. 2016 CONTRASTS: Nuts and Bolts
22. 2017 CONTRASTS: Mothers and Fathers
23. 2018 CONTRASTS: Now and Then

The *Plateau Area Writers Quarterly* began as an eight-page newsletter in 1999, with member contributions, and has grown to a twenty-page publication including items of Program speakers, a President's Corner, information about critique, creative groups, and member activity. There are stories, memoirs, and poems written by members, ranging in age from middle school to 90s. We encourage you to join us as a writer, as a subscriber, or an advertiser. The Quarterly is available to libraries through EBSCOhost electronically.

-- Paul T. Jackson, Editor

Now and Then
Some Are Called

There becomes a time, now and then,
a situation where one is called to choose,
make a choice to do or die knowing
well doing so will alter all that will be
ever after as they leave behind whatever was
to enter a new realm of possibility.
It is times like this that make a difference,
that are unimaginable as real life,
consequences, which occur because
one stepped up to the plate and made
a exclusive difference, crossed a line
of no return, embraced the cause,
the consequence in its effect. Is it bravery,
heroism, or just an ordinary person
being extra-ordinary? Thing that anyone
would do being at the point right there
where circumstance require participation?
Is it so that any human would have
the overwhelming urge to leap
directly to the task and apply whatever needs
intercession at a time there is no going back?
Is it divine intervention they are there
to intercede? What is it urges them to proceed
to risk without reward with no compulsion
otherwise, no hesitation just because they are?
Is it at that time the mere motivation
is being human that leaps them up
to the forefront with instinctive survival

of the species in their needs to thrust them
into causes to which they react, do not retreat.
How is it they are where they are, making them
the anointed ones given all the twists and turns
they could pursue, they could have taken
before that time sending them far away
from the very place they are, moment, need,
the very place they are. The event that called
upon their unabashed reality to be the appointed one?
This is not to say they act alone, for many time
there are others who are equal to the need,
spontaneously jump in to support, react, and gladly follow
the first responder with the frenzy of adrenaline
that drives them all into their fate
and heat of the battle to do good?
How about the other ones? What drives them
from this fate as they turn and run and disappear?
Which one would we become given us a chance?

Then and Now

Then I used the clutch in changing gears,
Now my left foot has no task to do;
Low oil then among our greatest fears,
Computers now note *Maintenance is due.*

Then I rose to turn the channel knob,
Now I sit and click on the remote;
Five channels made my choice an easy job,
Now hundreds of them lobby for my vote.

Then I typed a letter, folded twice
To fit the envelope that I addressed;
Now I need not worry a stamp's price:
Email goes for free; I guess I'm blessed.

And yet no matter what new things accrue,
My hours yet race by, and ever are too few.
No matter the technology we hail,
We'll get the ancient message: *System fail.*

© 2018, James F. O'Callaghan

Now And Then We Find

Now and then is what eternity fulfills
by will and by design that none escape
for living now and then but by not so
subtle means and sublime circumstance
the grand motion leads imperceptibly
from one end of the other now and then
leaving us to fate and finally a destiny.

THINGS AND SUCH

© June 1, 2017. A. Louise Deffley

Just lately, I've been taking stock of what I once thought of as my belongings. Don't get me wrong, they are still mine, but lately I view them as my things. Somehow, that seems a bit more up-to-date.

A few years back, when I was taking a grief counseling class, I discovered many of the younger generation called all things "stuff." Oh my, would it be possible for me to ever think of my treasured belongings as 'stuff'? My answer seemed a positive 'no' until I looked closer at some of my things.

I looked at the little items my children had made years ago. True, they are falling apart. Does that make them stuff? More than likely to some people, but not to me! I still remember the eager face that handed me that piece of bark with tiny ferns and small stones glued on to it. Can it be that little heart-felt thing is stuff? I hold it close and put it back on the shelf.

Next I notice the river rock with a glued-on smaller rock painted like a face. That one had graced my desk as a paperweight for all the years following the time a vice-president gave it to me for Christmas one year. Perry is gone now these many years. I have glued the face back on more times than I can remember. Surely, that is stuff. I smile and put it back on the shelf.

That funny little china mouse holding a birthday cake with one candle catches my attention. One ear is chipped. I'll just add it to the things that are really stuff. Placing it in the go box, I remember Lois and that she is also no longer here. It was cancer of the throat that took my long-ago friend. We had such interesting birthday lunches together. I place it carefully back on the shelf.

The shelf of music boxes certainly has more value than stuff. I add them to my 'things' list. Of course, you understand each holds a precious memory of the time and place I received it.

Then there are the family treasures. Some may be valuable. Certainly Uncle Jim's hunting horn would be a collectable by anyone who enjoys history.

The teapot with cups and plates was a wedding gift. My silver brandy snifter, a gift from co-workers, brings back more memories. My only problem with these is just who will own them one day when I'm no longer in possession. Will they cherish them as I have? Why should I worry about such things as that?

In the bedroom, it appears as if I have too many shoes. There are several pairs that haven't been on my feet for years. Surely, they are stuff – or things – or belongings? I have a difficult foot to fit. Maybe I'd better keep them.

I puzzle on further in to the bedroom. The closet doesn't hold many things I do not currently wear. I do weed the closet out on a regular basis due mainly to the space allowed.

The drawers hold even more things. Personal items hide there. When all else fails me, I tuck whatever I don't know exactly what to do with into a drawer. At times it could be just any drawer. It'll take some doing to sort those out.

I notice my musical jewelry box really holds nothing valuable. It takes up about a third of one drawer. It seems I have no other place to put it. It was a gift from Don. Of course it is a thing.

The bed makes a comfortable place to ponder it all. I perch there to reflect. The young person who talked about her 'stuff' included everything she owned in the world in her remark. She only left out her car. Could all my belongings – my things – be just 'stuff' to others?

Oreo cookies have stuff between the layers. Some even have double stuff. Then again, I've heard people talk about discussing stuff and nonsense. Maybe this is all nonsense after all. All that I survey is mine – or Don's, my husband. To me there is no stuff here – things maybe – belongings certainly. Then again, I discover to me they are treasures all.

Liberty

(A chapter from 'Cowboy Bob')
by Larry Krackle

Fall of 1969, our English teacher, Mrs. Koch, greeted us as we entered her class. "Today, there will not be a lesson. The draft lottery is being announced on the radio. It just started." She turned up the radio volume. The room became deathly silent. Every student waited in anticipation.

The announcer picked a capsule out of the bin, opened it and broadcast a number that represented a birth date.

Two-hundred sixty-four."

Everyone breathed a sigh of relief.

"Seventy-six."

Darrell groaned and slumped in his chair. "March seventeen. My birthday."

An hour later, when most numbers had been announced, "One hundred and one," came over the airwaves.

I jumped up and clapped. "Whoo-Hoo! April eleven. I got a high number."

After school, I ran all the way home. I whooped as I burst into the house.

Mom looked up from the kitchen table. "What's going on?"

"My draft number 325 was picked. That means I'll be one of the last to go out of my class."

A sober expression clouded Dad's face. "You should be proud to serve your country."

"Not in Viet Nam. It isn't even a war. The government is forcing us kids to go fight and kill."

"You're being unpatriotic."

"No I'm not. I just don't agree with his war. I'm only seventeen. I can't vote. I can't drink or smoke."

"I hope you never do," said Mom, "go to war, drink, or smoke."

"Sit down." Dad beckoned to a chair. "Let me tell you a story."

"After boot camp in California, I boarded a train and headed across country. We were on the way to war in Europe. All along the way people waved. They gave us goodies and drinks. We arrived at Camp Kilmer, New Jersey, four days later. After being assigned to barracks, we waited."

And waited.

Then the great day for embarkation came. We were issued full field packs, uniforms and boots. They bused us out to the dock and marched us up the gangplank. I didn't appreciate the old English ship with only hammocks to sleep in. The food was lousy. When land finally disappeared from view, all I could see was the ocean. From horizon to horizon. There was more water than I had ever seen. Coming out of North Dakota, this country boy was not at all pleased.

It made me nervous when the escort ships dropped depth charges. There were about seventy-five ships. Two lines of troop ships. An aircraft carrier sailed to the left. To the right were oil tankers and cruisers. It was an impressive sight. They never changed positions except those small craft that rolled barrels off the back. They went boom and our ship shuddered.

It took two weeks because of the route we took. We ate meals at the rear of the ship from our mess kits. That wasn't so bad until I attempted to wash my kit in hot salt water. The throbbing of the motors was too much. I didn't throw up but I had to make about three attempts to get my kit clean.

We disembarked at Liverpool, England. They marched us through the countryside to old military grounds near Salisbury. Ten or more hospital units camped there. Everyone slept in tents, waiting to be assigned.

The first thing I did was look for fellow church boys. Fortunately, I finally found one. He gave the address of a home church. So my first leave, I took off for Sunday Morning Meeting. I arrived on Saturday afternoon and stayed at their home.

This was an eye-opener for me. To be a stranger another country and they received me with open arms. Very righteous English people.

While in that camp, I rode my bike to Salisbury and cycled past the famous Stonehenge.

Finally we got orders to move. They bussed us south to Yeovilton Army Post in Somerset County. We set up our 159th General Hospital. By then I was just a ward boy. Not that I liked it but one doesn't always do what they like.

We set up our hospital and received patients. The first night was a complete fill up. The work began. Bed pans, urinals, wash clothes, bed baths, enemas, and griping. One of my patients was a young kid. He was in a private room with wounds on every limb. One leg was slit to the bone from inside of leg to knee. I didn't know that until the doctor took the bandage off. I won't describe it further.

The doctor told me "Maybe you better stick your head out the window for some fresh air."

The smell of gangrene is putrid. We saved him and he gave me the worst time of any.

There was another kid who never really went to battle but got hit with a German 88 flak shell. The gun was an anti-aircraft used as ground fire toward Allied troops. He was in traction with pins in both knees and a nasty wound in his upper leg.

They introduced maggots to eat the dead flesh. One day while feeling around his leg, he found the maggots. End of maggots for him.

Then one time about five of us went to London. We had a good time even though the sirens blew and a few rockets exploded. It scared the daylights out of me. Lucky I didn't go to France. I'd still be running.

Spring of 1944, the Normandy invasion took place. Our hospital filled to overcapacity with injured. Then the Allies declared victory. I was in one victory parade. We marched with the British men and women at their pace. It's at one hundred twenty, almost twice as fast as our march-step.

Then the officers closed the camp. I gave my bicycle to an English friend. They bused us up to Scotland and we boarded the Queen Elizabeth. We had fifteen thousand people on board. Thirty-six men were assigned to a boardroom for two. Half slept on deck or wherever we found space. We didn't need an alarm clock, because those crazy sailors swabbed the decks down with powerful hoses at five o'clock.

I didn't get seasick on the way back home. The fresh salt air was like perfume compared to the hospital odors of medicine and rotting flesh. I still get anxiety going to the doctor. It reminds me of my nursing days in the military.

Halfway across the ocean a storm blew in from the west. The sea is fantastic by looking out on the sides. It seemed that about ten or twenty acres of water would just rise up to incredible heights. Then it would collapse into a swale. I was glad to be in a seaworthy vessel.

A week later, the captain announced that New York would come into view shortly. Everyone crowded to the bow of the ship. The Statue of Liberty looked magnificent after fourteen months away from America. There wasn't a dry eye on deck."

Dad finished by saying, "I'm proud to have served my country. I hope you have a change of heart."

My bubble burst. I still had negative feelings about the Viet Nam war. Recently, a friend came back in a body bag. Several kids at school protested. I felt like joining them but they were looked down upon as troublemakers.

Two months later, a letter came in the mail from the U.S. government. With trembling hands I opened it. The message instructed me to report to the nearest recruiting station and register.

"What's the letter say?" Mom asked.

"I gotta go register."

"When?"

"Within the month."

She took her sweater from a clothes hook. "Might as well get it out of the way. Let's go."

We jumped in the car and drove to Aberdeen. Four nervous boys fidgeted in the waiting room when we entered. Just babies. I took a number and waited.

A man in uniform called out. "Laurence?"

"That's me." I walked to his desk and sat down.

He gave me several forms to fill out. One line asked for the name of a university. I quickly printed 'Grays Harbor Community College.'

After registering, we walked out of the building and jumped in the car.

"I'm going to college," I said.

Mom looked surprised. "You're going to college?"

"Yes."

"What brought that on?"

"I can get a deferment. With my high draft number combined, I most likely won't have to go to Viet Nam."

Mom breathed a sigh of relief. "I'm glad, but don't tell Dad. It disturbs him."

When Veteran's Day came, Dad put a large American flag on the front porch. Once the staff was firmly placed in the post bracket, he stood back and saluted.

He turned to me. "A lot of blood has been shed for our freedom."

"Boys are dying in vain today against their own will," I argued.

"And your college friends are dying for a worthless cause too. You'll get no tuition money from me if you become an anti-war demonstrator."

I flashed him the two-finger peace sign. "So be it."

"Only the patriotic are welcome in my home." He turned and marched into the house.

I felt like he was poking me about my views of the Viet Nam

war. Three more friends were killed. One came back wounded. He told me horror stories of the campaign, or lack of it. They'd take a hill, then evacuate. The Viet Cong would recapture the area. This went on and on.

A year later I left home to attend Washington State University. Since I now lived on the opposite side of the state, distance helped reduce the friction between my Father and me. Anti-war demonstrations took place daily on campus. Rioters burned the flag and their draft cards. Five of my friends moved to Canada. I don't ever recall anyone being disrespectful of someone in the military.

Many Baby Boomers turned twenty-one and became eligible to vote. Politicians, fearing for their positions, started voting against war issues. In 1973 the draft was discontinued. A heavy burden shed from my back. Dad seemed to be relieved also.

Dad specified in his will that I would receive his military burial flag. When he passed, I accepted it, proud of him for serving his country. Even though I am still anti-war, I believe in a strong military and am very patriotic.

Our 20th history notes

The present Plateau Area Writers Roster
[Second Quarter 1999-from March meeting]

Miriam Bowers
Betty Brown
Sue Berner
Dick Brugger
Geneva Burgess
Alpha Butcher
Louise Deffley
Lady Dyar
Elaine Estes
Robert Gaylord
Lisa Godfrey-Abts
Carol Lynn Harp
Dorothea Kreklow,
Emmy Knemeyer
Sharon Mack
Pat McGaw
Alisa Nickels
Jeff Opheim
Rueben Powell
Jean Richardson
Ward Roberts
Cardine Saint
Heidi Shelton
Ruth Stepetin
Nan Wright
Betty York

Our 20th history notes

Plateau Area Writers Association Officers
[Second Quarter, Summer 1999]

Chairman
> Robert Gaylord

Vice chairman
> Carol Lynn Harp

Recorder
> Emmy Knemeyer

Correspondence Officer
> Sue Berner

Finance Officer
> Reuben Powell

Outreach Programs Officer
> Jeff Opheim

Quarterly Editor
> Richard Brugger

Assistant Editor
> Louise Deffley

Our 20th history notes

1999 – 3rd Quarter By-Laws

Rueben Powell, Jeff Opheim and Robert Gaylord
Architects of the PAWA by-laws.

Officers 2000 Summer Quarterly

Chairman:
>   Robert Gaylord

Vice chairman.
>   Carol Lynn Harp

Recorder
>   Louise Deffley
>   Emmy Knemeyer

Correspondence Officer
>   Sue Berner

Finance Officer
>   Reuben Powell

Outreach Programs Officer
>   Jeff Opheim

Quarterly Editor
>   Richard Brugger

Assistant Editor
>   Louise Deffley

Our 20th history notes

Critique Groups: Summer 2000

Founders and original Group

Foothills Writers - Met at Bob's Baker Street Bookstore
  Sue Berner, Miriam Bowers, Elaine Estes, Louise Deffley
Emmy Knemeyer, Jeff Opheim, Ruth Stepetin.
    Sadly, this first critique group, formed in 1998, will no longer be meeting; Retired 2017. Accolades for their perseverance to the remaining two members, Louise Deffley and Miriam Bowers now retiring.
Baker Street Writers - Met at Baker Street Bookstore
  Carol Lynn Harp, Dorothea Kreklow, Reuben Powell,
Heidi Shelton.
Green River Writers Guild - Met in Auburn
        Dick Brugger, Geneva Burgess, Alpha Butcher,
Robert Gaylord

Over the years we've had numbers of groups:
        Former groups:
Covington Poetry Group
The Egg & I — Enumclaw Friday breakfast creative group
Poetry Jam — meeting at Arts Alive and Sequel Books, Enumclaw
Writers in the Woods —Creative/Flash writing group. Started at
  Muckleshoot Library, Auburn, ended at Puyallup library.
Puyallup Critique Group— Meeting in Puyallup Library.
Dennis Keene Scriptwriters -- Enumclaw
Krain Novel writers—Enumclaw
Tree House Novel writers —Auburn Treehouse
Sci-Fi /Novel writers—Puyallup

Memories

I stand in the now,
Overlooking the places in time
Where I've been.

I pull up the happy memories.
I smile, I laugh,
I feel a sweet warmth in my heart.
I know what to do with these.
I put them on the walls of my mind
To look at often,
To take down when I need to smile.

I pull up the tearful memories,
The bittersweet of times gone by.
I hold the intangible touch of
Loved ones past, and loved ones lost.
I know what to do with these.
I put these in a treasure box in my mind
To pull out at precious times
That remind me of their qualities;
To surround me in their warmth.

I pull up shameful memories.
I wonder what to do with these.
They feel prickly to the touch,
And make my hand recoil.
I want to throw them all away.
But wait.
Is there a reason they are here?
I pick one up and see a tear.
I peel the skin.
The hard outer crust, I find,
Holds treasures underneath.

Great treasures most important not to toss.
Here a layer of learning,
Next a layer of understanding,
A layer of growth,
One of knowledge, wisdom too!

Oh I know what to do with these.
Unpeel each prickly memory
And make them all a part of me.

© 3/14/2007, Jana Nielsen

Surrounded by Trees...
This Home

Now, something must be written
Some record left of our *being*
Record of our being *here*
Of living out a life
Living long life
In this place
This particular *place*

Across time
The *mystery* of time
Seeds from ancient trees
Germinate, root, grow, *live*
A few years or a hundred
Die, decay, become soil
To welcome seedlings
In this *place*

What new trees
Will be nurtured here
In the soil that was our life
Long, long life?
Life amazing filled with
Not merely fear, anxiety, anger, angst,
But wonder

Hope, faith, love
Emanating from this *place*
Love, faith, hope
Love.......love   love

© 2018, Isabel Brady Jackson

Now and Then a Memory Reviewed

Sometimes my mind relinquishes a memory
from the depths of years for my review,

and I feel my breath catch in my throat
as thoughts and emotions collide
when reminiscence is triggered
by an incident, a sight, a sound,
a scent, perhaps a touch.

The grasp of memories takes hold
and brings back people and places joined
to the past I cannot revisit except by review,
for time transforms space, and lost moments
cannot be reclaimed.

A certain glow of summer light, or a frost etching
made by the hand of winter on my window glass
before star shine, or the crumble of spent autumn leaves
under foot, and I am there again as are you.

Then I feel the loss of moments and hours,
previously thought of as routine,
part of those seemingly infinite days of ennui
once shared.

Time to Let Things Go

What I have is not quite feeling right?
I used to be precise and anymore I can't
quite get up to speed. Seems I've slipped
a cog or two in the old timing chain.
Maybe one of my cylinders has burned
a hole or the head blown a gasket
and the valves not seating tight, the
cam shaft worn a flat spot. Nothing
is the same as the former me filled with
my young energy. Perhaps that is OK.
What need I to further be at the top
of this game? I like to sit listening now
 to the weather passing through,
close my eyes, and think of all the things

I let slip by and all the ones that I did not
That now made my memories. I used to be
a full-agenda guy with every moment filled,
productive, getting things all done. Now
I'd rather sit and scratch the cat to see
if he will purr and think of what I next
might write to tell about my life, but then that
is an awful lot to think about, the years
and years back then and the words now
I wish to use don't quite fit the lines.
Better still I'd rather let the randomness
fill my time instead of me filling up this page
with rhyme and unreasonable reason, be impulsive
to the minute as I wait for the next
impulse to stick and be my motivation
to get up and move. Maybe fix another
cup of joe to sip and sit and think on what
there is next to not do as on and on I age.

WHEN I GROW UP

© 2017, Paul T. Jackson

When I tell people of all the things I've done during my eighty-three years of life, they say, "My, you've certainly had an interesting life," and at one point in my fifties, one person said, "You're not old enough to have done that much," to which I usually reply, "Yes, I'm still trying to figure out what I want to be when I grow up."

In a way, I suspect, I was saying this because it would bring some smiles and maybe a few laughs from time to time, but in "retirement" it seems to mean to some on hearing it; "I didn't have a very good career track," or "I wonder why he couldn't keep a job?"

I think my father found out the answer to the latter question when my aunt rescued me from my father, critical of my "career track". Her husband was a supervisor at Chrysler Motor Company and had to lay off many people from time to time, and my aunt told my dad how it was…you don't get a choice to stay. When a strike requires the money to be made up, companies unload older more expensive workers. When a store closes, a company gets sold, or union and management can't or won't solve a serious problem and people leave, people generally don't have the choices they would like to have.

On the other hand, there has been the idea, or value, if you will, having a single lifetime career like a lawyer, doctor, fireman, policeman, librarian, teacher, and so forth, is somehow more valuable than having several careers. Back in 1994, I believe it was John L. Peterson in his book, *The Road to 2015: Profiles of the Future*, predicted the future would see people with multiple careers… similar to my experience in the 60s through 90s. Perhaps I was experiencing what the future would be like. In fact, in 1959, I had met a man with a solid career position with Xerox and had held the job for ten years, but told me he was leaving. I asked him why and he responded, "I think life is too short to be spending it doing the same thing over and over and over." So even back then there were some who did not value a single career as sacrosanct.

The truth is, some people are never satisfied with the status quo, want to change it, or build upon it, something they can call their own. One minister suggested there were only two kinds of people; those who maintain, and those who build--although I was told by another there are really three kinds of people; those who can count and those who can't.

I suppose people who build those gigantic sand castles are builders of one sort; knowing their creation will fail and they can recreate something different each time. Other builders build for posterity, expecting their creations to survive and maybe get better over time--or at least leave the world a bit better than before. Artists, sculptors, writers—all—hope their works will continue to delight and help people. My many careers certainly have been about establishing new organizations, companies and libraries.

What will I be when I grow up? My multiple careers could be considered as just one, and the final epitaph on my grave might be "Builder." What will yours be?

Emerging

Sometimes it takes a life-time
Of uprooting oneself
Clearing out and holding
To emerge from the clay

My kayak flows on forgotten rivers
As sunlight bounces off the laughing
Ripples of liquid, where trees
Bow down to meet me

I find God here every time
I allow the river to carry me
I pull history from the bank
Smooth silky silt, a potter's friend

Closing my eyes, I drift
Knowing these days won't last
Forever and I take snap-shots in my mind;
breathing in the earthy smells of forest

A silver streak next to me, salmon
Eagle cries overhead and leaves
Of many colors swirl along with me
I hold this clay of God's work in image

Today I cannot lift a paddle nor
Hear the cry of an eagle but I can
Hold and mold the clay of memories
And little birds emerge from my hands

© 7/12/2018, Genora W. Powell

Just Give Me a Minute

And I'll tell you:
I'll tell you about my deck,
my deck that hangs above the ravine,
above the ravine where a little stream runs.
It runs still in spite of the knotweed,
the Japanese knotweed that spreads
along the banks of this seasonal rivulet.

I'll tell you about the deer wandering through
wandering through the tall stalks of living,
spreading knotweed and over the dead reeds
from last year's crop, last year's knotweed
reeds lying thick on the ravine floor, covering
seeds of daisies, marsh marigold, bloodroot.

I'll tell you how last autumn the
sprayer came,
the sprayer came the year before too and
the stand is smaller now; but now new plants,
little ones, are sprouting along the ravine bank
below my deck, my deck built around the magnificent

oak tree, <u>oak</u> tree, one hundred years old.

I'll tell you: Consider the oak tree, rooted just here,
rooted on the lip of this ravine;
now its top reaches seventy feet into the sky;
high in the air, it spreads its massive limbs
over my little house on the west bank,
massive branches splay beyond the house,
up, beyond and over, giving shade to bless my dwelling.

I'm telling you, blessing above, scourge below:
knotweed perhaps never to be eradicated, scourge forever;
the white oak, strong, healthy, yet vulnerable.
We will not give into resignation or despair,
we will fight to save our native plants--
the enemy: the exotic, toxic, pernicious interlopers.

I'll tell you, in spite of wild incursions
beyond our deck, below our oak, the weed,
yet our white oak stands, proud, strong, dignified,
reaches toward the heavens.
You gave me a minute and I've told you.

Only for Today

All my tomorrows
Have faded away
Now I live
Only in my today
For looking back
On my yesterdays
Brings me to
Realize I can't
Relive them,
I can't retrieve
The joy, though
I long too
I don't want
To recall anymore
Of the hell
Though, I want
To change them
All my tomorrows
Have faded away
I am now only
Living for today.

© 6/27/2018, Genora W. Powell

FILLING UP MY LIFE

This journal I write in is getting filled,
another of my ambitions to move my life
along, views documented as I go.
I must have twenty more or so of my life,
each page filled of a time and that day's
expressions noted but no idea the date
presented while my life sequenced through
as if I might someday make a difference
to you and if not that then someone unknown
in another life and time as my own ends
and they read where I have been now
and then along my long way through.

© 2018, Alan C Keimig

BEST FRIEND

© 1998, Robert S Gaylord

Juan Sepulveda is my best friend. Well, really he's my only friend. I guess he has been ever since he came to little 'ol Tustin High from the huge Santa Ana High School in our county seat of Orange County, California. I'm happy now I have a friend who is not embarrassed to make good grades and he's an athlete too.

Mom was Juan's teacher in the seventh grade and he was a favorite of hers. I sometimes wonder if she had anything to do with his transferring to Tustin High. Mom said that the Sepulvedas live on the district border. This means they have a choice of school districts. Tustin and Santa Ana are only three miles apart anyway and our little town blends into the big city under the arching arms of giant old walnut trees.

Coming to Tustin was a good thing for him too; he is a track star and a Big Man on Campus here. He recently won the lead part in our junior play. The girls like him, probably because he is handsome, with his wavy black hair, sparkling brown eyes and silky-smooth brown skin. The teachers like him too, he is very polite and works hard to get good grades.

Some boys and girls call me "Hunchback" because of my good grades. They don't seem to mind that Juan gets 'em too. Maybe Juan doesn't carry around all the books I do.

School is over today. Juan and I are strolling along the wide sidewalk they call The Alameda leading from high school to the Sunkist Packing Plant. Seeing the big old green wooden structure makes me think about when Juan and I worked at the packing plant last summer.

Juan helped me get the job loading the rail cars with boxes of oranges packed and ready for shipment. It was hard work but I liked working with all the energetic Mexicans. The guys were always acting macho and the gals worked hard at wrapping the oranges and forcing them into boxes for shipment. They seem to jabber and laugh all the time.

One gal often brought a bunch of tasty little sandwich things she called *burritos* to sell at work. They were stuffed with vegetables like green beans or potatoes and wrapped in thin flour pancakes she called *tortillas*. I always bought some; they are delicious!

Juan's usual job last summer was to unload field boxes as they are brought into the plant from the orange orchards that surround us in every direction. One day he showed me how to unload the boxes from the flatbed trucks and dump their contents onto the conveyer belt. It is really hard to do; they are super heavy and they are stacked seven high. I could barely reach the top box. I'm glad that wasn't my job every day!

I worked in the underground refrigerator room helping the guys put boxes of the right grade of packed oranges onto the conveyor belt that goes out to the rail cars. My main job was to tally the number of boxes of each grade for the manifest. The tally-man job pays quite a bit better than the other jobs in the plant.

Awakening from my daydream of last summer, I turned to Juan, "Come on home with me Juan. We can have supper together. Mom would like to see you. After supper we can blow some jazz for awhile."

The bushes along the public walk are overgrown; they push out onto the path. The white star blooms fill the air with a perfume that both blends and conflicts with the ever-present orange blossoms. Juan swats at the dark green limbs as he thinks about my offer.

"OK, Bobby, but I must be home by eight. That's when Mom gets back from her new job. I'm hoping my Dad will come over tonight, his combo is playing nearby, in Stanton." Juan smiles at the thought of his dad visiting home.

As far as I've seen, his dad is always gone from home. Juan has said he is playing guitar in various roadhouses around Southern California and on down into Baja California. I know Juan would want to see his dad if there was a chance, but I'm sure playing our piano again is a strong attraction to come over for awhile.

"Come on, I'll race ya'," I blurted out, mixed with laughter.

Running hard down Sixth Street toward my home, Juan has passed me and is well in the lead. We are both still laughing at this ridiculous race. He's a star athlete in high hurdles. Not only are we slapping the road with our shoes but the doves are slapping too. They are flying up from the street where they have been eating the walnuts crushed in the road. It is quite a scene; birds' going everywhere with wings slapping together as they rise.

Seems like every house along Sixth Street has either an old walnut tree in the front yard or an avocado tree arching out over the road. Their dark green leaves provide much needed shade in our perpetual summer.

Suddenly Juan stops running and picks up a ripe avocado from the ground. I smile as I truly love avocados. He hands it to me. I caress the wrinkled black skin as I cut it in half with my pocketknife and pop the seed out. We walk along eating our fresh avocado when someone shouts at us in Spanish:

" Toe May Low " is what it sounds like. I don't understand.

" *Sace lo*", Juan shouts back.

Juan stands in the road with his hands on his hips looking at the boys who shouted. He waves them off with laughter, turns and is now jogging up the road. I am running to keep up with him. I ask him between gasps, "What was that about?"

"Just insults; it's not important."

"Why do those guys insult you Juan, I've noticed it at school?"

"I'm Spanish, a heritage hated by some Mexicans. Their people were Peons…farm workers…and Indios. The Spanish were landowners. Los Indios tell stories of mistreatment at the hands of the landowners and the church. Some still want to remember those times."

Juan is walking again. He turns and smiles, pulling a ripe

orange off the tree next to my home and continues; "More important probably, is the fact that my folks spoke very little Spanish in our home. They wanted the children to speak English well. I can't really speak Spanish, especially not the slang spoken around here." I duck as an orange peel bounces off my shoulder.

"But Juan, you answered those guys."

"Yeah, I know some of the slang insults…my dad told me."

As we walk up the driveway to my home I feel Juan is like a man without a country. Is it also partly because we are pals? Are there three reasons some of the kids act like they do; he is proud of his Spanish heritage, but doesn't speak Spanish, and his pal is gringo.

"Hi Mom," Juan says.

I look up and see my Mom in the doorway. I'm glad Juan says this. I'm glad he feels this way about my mom. She is opening the door, hugging Juan and saying that dinner will be ready soon.

I run and get my clarinet hollering over my shoulder; "Hey, you just got to see my new clarinet. Take a look at the beautiful wood. This is not the tin horn from the high school band, this has tone! I am learning to play clarinet just as well as my sax. You have to blow 'em both to be professional. Listen, I'll play some old-style jazz."

I finger out a few mellow tones, playing the verse, *Do you know what it means to miss New Orleans?* I put the instrument down in the stand beaming with pride, "I've decided, jazz is my life. The Jazz band gives me a place. I'm a real professional musician. People clap their hands and yell when I finish a riff, or take a ride, you know; when I improvise a solo. Playing in a big band puts me in another world. I get away from all the high school kids' crap."

Bubbling with enthusiasm I continue, "performances are a visit to wonderland. It's like a trip to Oz, man. We hear our recordings afterwards. We listen and dream of being studio musicians."

Juan is showing interest so I keep talking, "I wish you'd join us Juan. You'd be good for us. Then you'd know what it's like to be part of the full sound. It's in the groove; you'd love it. Come with me tomorrow and try out with the *Blue Notes*, we don't have a regular piano. Have you heard of us? The band started with a bunch of high school and college kids from Santa Ana and Tustin. We called ourselves the *Blue Notes*. We were pretty good even without a leader."

I watched Juan's face to see if he was still interested.

"Then Gordon heard us and took over as the leader. He changed everything. He got us a lot of new music and now we practice over at the college. Gordon's a professor or something. He knows the business, for sure. He gets us a lot of work. Hey, our new word is gigs. We get a lot of gigs! Even our rehearsals have a lot of people coming and watching us now!"

Mom tells us to wash up and get ready to eat. I help Dad put an extra leaf in the table and Dad changes the subject to sports. Dad used to coach Juan in high hurdles and they have common interests.

After dinner we go into the living room. Juan is running his fingers around on the piano, playing parts of various tunes. I'm sure he doesn't get to play a piano very often. He's pretty good, good enough anyway to put great chords together and score jazz music. I am amazed he can play this well without any lessons. I took piano lessons, trumpet lessons and finally tried the sax. The sax is my love. It is a lot easier fingering than any other instrument.

Juan is working on a new arrangement of *I Only Have Eyes for You*. I help with some of the harmony. I can score the trumpet section and sax section. He knows the trombone and rhythm sections. He already has the sheets together for base, piano and drums. We are fully absorbed in scoring a jazz version for a big band. It takes a lot of sheets. We're crawling all over the floor writing notes on paper and I suddenly realize he's got to get home.

42

I yell, "Mom, can I borrow your car and take Juan home?"

I turn to Juan, "I like to drive mom's car, Dad's old pickup is too hokey."

We drive in silence along Second Street toward Santa Ana. Juan is looking at the sky, "What a pretty night; it isn't very often you can see the Milky Way."

I thought, *You really mean it isn't very often you get to see your dad.*

I turn into the driveway; "Hope you're not too late and didn't miss your dad. See you tomorrow. Think about the band."

As I back out the drive, I see the man that must be his dad come to the door.

The next day Juan is not in school. That evening he doesn't show for our rehearsal.

Today he's back at school I chide him, "Hey Juan why didn't you come by the college and try out for the band? You could at least listen to us rehearse. Get a free concert."

Juan smiles and says, "I did stop by and listen for awhile, my dad took me over. You were so deep into the music it was a waste to bother you."

"What did you think?" I asked, hoping to get approval. "Did you hear us play your arrangement of, *I Only Have Eyes for You?*"

"Your band is pretty good. I was excited to hear how far along you have come in developing the full sound intended. I am also excited…my dad wants me to play piano with his combo. We're going to tour all over. Isn't this great? You're in a big band and I'm going to play with my dad!"

After a long pause, I start to come to grips with what he is saying; "You're serious? Does this mean you'd leave school?"

"I would still go to school between gigs and in places where the gig lasts long enough. Our first set is in The Baja, Bobby, now I can be a *Mexican.*"

What the Middle West is Like

Out here in this vast display of emptiness
the radio plays its loneliness, every
song a new testament to
a lonesome time driving through
the night between coming and going
penetrated only by the noise of
crickets and heartbreak that covers
them in dark and ties on the road
here and there punctuated by a house
with light coming from a lone window,
then a single row of trees running
windward south to north , beyond
them, fields and field as far as
all their imagination stretched in
the mystic moonlight making all
seem more magical than real
growing taller by the stars at night
and day the day chore as little rain
will stunt and gray growth per usual
just as the singing too says so
for all the work so little gain
as morning begins to break behind
my driving west away onward
further into the days lighting display
where I will suffer and survive
finding at some end ahead enough
to make the leaving all worthwhile.
the staying still another lonely day.

© Alan C. Keimig

TRYING TO RECOVER ME

When I feel the mood now and then
I walk beyond the places humans made
into the pristine wilderness to roam
where no worn path leads, led solely
by my walk's authority in woods,
up hills and mountain sides, alongside
a quiet pool and near the roar
of a falling waterfall to sit alone
for time to have the stillness enter me
beside the absent work of mortal hands
while I wait held face to face with nature
now to see what it will have me know about
myself and notice what it will tell me then
in the quiet company I find with my spirit
held, my heart renewed, my mind restored.

© 2018, Alan C Keimig

WONDERFUL LIFE

I often think about my wonderful life
Blessed by God, whom I needed often.

Camping out, hunting, fishing enjoyments
With my wonderful father, out in the woods

I played baseball in high school, batted .420
St. Louis Cardinal's recruiter asked me to join them.

I decided college was far more important
There I studied hard, received scholarships.

Left college to work in El Segundo, California
I enjoyed America's new rockets and space business

Travelling around the world in science,
Presented creative papers often, world-wide

Next I was assigned to Washington, D.C.
I was promised I would become a VP.

If I built up business there in D.C.
I worked hard contacting all job possibilities.

We did build up business with many agencies,
And next I obtained our own secure facilities.

Business expanded to the goals as set,
We had lots of people with work to do.

Then I was asked to move back to El Segundo
Surprised, sold my Virginia house and returned.

Three Vice Presidents replaced me in D.C.
A surprising disappointment, to say the least

The CEO forced my retirement from El Segundo
I was embittered by all the lies he told me

Then, many companies got in touch with me
I consulted with industry for two years: fun jobs!

Once invited to lunch with business folks
Standing applause greeted me as I appeared.

Also worked tirelessly from home for Celsat
Made nothing for this effort, CEO was a buddy.

Then went to college again, I studied much about
Creative writing, was different from engineering.

Completely retired, I helped form a non-profit of
Creative writers where I was elected President.

We named it Plateau Area Writers' Association
I enjoyed making my own business cards.

In total I was President of PAWA for eleven years,
Then, retired again, I heard applause from PAWA.

End game joy is being published by PAWA
Both in their newspapers and books

I worked long hours writing stories,
It made me feel I really wasn't retired.

Looking back now, it was a wonderful life.
I thank God for all my blessings.

© 1/12/2018, R. S. Gaylord

When Dreams Become the New Reality

Alert, optimistic, and still mortal to
the dark deep calling of the ocean home
we crawled out from into this anchored
madness called human life I joined the core.
But then there are the dreams that catch us
sinking down into the cold oblivion
of our kind and I too am not immune
as then at the last cold minute I like others are
buoyed up to the surface of deep sleep to survive
jarred awake into a conscious consequence.
Now I find myself waiting for the next new round
of words to embark upon my mind, arrange
and rearrange then loose themselves into a range
of bizarre concepts filtered in against reality
so bruised and banged it takes a bent coat hanger
shoved down inside the crack to unlatch the locked
existence arranged with a slight semblance of new hope
for a work in progress, a series of ideas which can align
the day into four clear segments carefully defined
with clear cut lines which are not fog into each other.
There is an indication here that what it is above
all-else seems to have as definite a fit in my life's scheme
And if not that then abiding by expectation borne
of life's first submissions climbing up to the shore
mildly disfigure with arms and legs for all intentions
before this has become the end with dreams as they
become fixations with new truth to increasingly live by.

SOME MORNINGS

Some mornings I leave bed
before I'm quite awake.
I rush around so I
get ready for a group
or to complete some tasks
before later meetings.

My brain is foggy and
my eyes don't focus well.
In my sleepiness and
haste, I may drop things, spill
things, mess things up. Then
I try to clean them up
And make even more messes.

On other mornings, I
lie in bed, sleeping and
dozing until I've had
enough rest. Then I can
cheerfully start my day.
Leisurely I do each
morning activity.
I plot the time ahead
recall what I have done.
My plans go smoothly then.

Why don't I always do
this? I would miss the groups.

[Normative syllabic verse]
© 08/25/2014, Carol Lynn Harp

APPLE CORE

© 2018, Robert Gaylord

I didn't expect an apple to reveal so much about my Dad as that little yellow apple did on that warm, fall afternoon at Dad's old home place in Paisley, Oregon. Dad had walked to the far end of our harvested alfalfa field to chat with our neighbor, Martha, who seemed to be puttering around in her apple orchard. I shuffled along through the alfalfa stubble to catch up with my dad. As I approached Dad and Martha, I could see some of the heavily-laden apple branches were over on our side of the fence and some apples were on the ground.

Martha said, "would you like some apples?"

Without hesitation Dad picked an apple up off the ground and bit right into it!

Martha said, "George, you better look out, there may be a worm in that apple!"

Dad said, "The worm better look out!"

I suddenly felt really embarrassed by his funny comment.

Martha laughed and laughed. I was pleased she did not seem to be as shocked and embarrassed as I was. I picked up an apple and checked it carefully for signs of wormholes. I bit into it gingerly. It was good. The rich aroma of a ripe Granny Smith apple filled my senses. I could tell my stomach was eager to get to work on that delicious apple!

We thanked Martha, picked up a few more apples, stuffed them in our pockets and started walking back across the field toward our house. I enjoyed walking along in the hot afternoon sun, eating an apple with my dad. At times, here in Oregon, his humor made it seem like he was still a kid. I loved to be here where he grew up. I could always learn more about my father when we were in Paisley.

"Is it OK to toss this apple core over there in the pasture, or will it make the horses sick?" I wondered out loud. I had heard stories of horses getting sick from eating green apples. Apparently, they get bloated to the point where someone has to stick a knife into the horse to relieve the pressure. I knew that job would be my responsibility if a horse got sick from my apple! I did not want to do that.

I wondered what Dad had done -- Oh my gosh, I could see he had eaten the entire apple, core and all!

He turned to me and suggested I do the same.

Right then and there I felt my mom was right: whenever she was angry at dad she would often say he was just a dang ol' Indian! He was so different in many ways, especially when we were out here in the country at our old home place.

I tossed my apple core out in the field, I felt surely, the horses would not get sick from such a ripe apple.

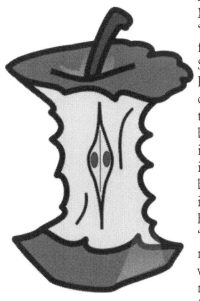

As we approached the house Mom hollered out the window, "Robbie, go pump some water for me, please."
Shucks, I'll tell you, none of us liked this chore. It was a difficult task for us kids pumping the water up two hundred feet, by cranking on the old fashioned pump. We couldn't carry it over to the house in the big bucket without spilling some of it, either. Mom knew it was a hated chore and often used, *"Go pump some water,"* as punishment, when one of her boys were misbehaving. This summer I was staying around home for once and not working on

nearby ranches, the way we kids usually did. So it usually fell on me to pump the water. I did love to stay at home where I could go rabbit hunting or fishing anytime that Dad didn't need help around the ranch.

I was happy the family has been coming to Oregon the last few summers. I heard this is because Mom and Dad are teachers and so they don't get paid in the summer, a time when school is out. Dad can find plenty of work here.

A couple of years ago we started coming back to the ranch where Dad was born and grew up. We got in the car and drove all the long way, as soon as school let out. Dad could always find carpenter work around town.

I began helping him this summer. There is quite a bit I can do now that I'm fourteen. We have already torn down an old barn and salvaged most of the wood. Then we shingled the roof of the general store. It was hard work for me, carrying the bundles of shingles up the ladder to Dad. Even so, I wanted to help with all his jobs around town because it was more fun to be with Dad in the summer. He seemed to go through a metamorphosis when we all got out on the road. He was more playful and would even sing weird songs along stretches of old highway 395. We kids didn't see much to be joyful about, while we were passing cactus, yucca, juniper, and miles upon miles of the ever-present sage bushes. Our old nineteen-thirty-six Chevy seemed pretty crowded with the four of us, a dog, and a cat. So when we stopped and camped evenings, in wooded areas with streams running through the wild roses and aspen groves it was very restful, even though we were all sleeping on the ground in Dad's home-made sleeping bags.

It took us three days driving north from Southern California to get to Paisley, Oregon, to our father's family old home place. But it seemed Dad knew how to make the time pass quickly by his singing and interesting comments about the surrounding terrain. Summers were, for me, a special education about country life and my father's true personality.

Chance Encounter Now And Then

I saw you once and then again
several days gone by and then
a third time when you glanced
my way and smiled, I smiled back
glad you too had recognized me
from an apparent passing chance before
in a world of six billion inhabitants
as I wonder how these things come to be
given all the calculated options
and the odds of these events and yet here
we are eye to eye, never a word spoken
as we pass through each other's life
as instances in time then and now
and the million more to still occur
in the random sequence as I wonder
who will be the next I will observe and they
too notice me as we catch each other's eyes
in déjà vu just so we notice now and then.

© 2018, Alan C Keimig

DRESS CODE—HATS

© 2018, Don Hagen

In the 1980s, there was a lot of concern about gang activity in South King County and the Auburn School District. We were required to attend workshops designed to teach us how to recognize the trappings of gang wear. Certain colors, hand signs, and articles of clothing were indices of gang activity. One indication of gang activity was the wearing of hats, sometimes worn in ways that delineated gang affiliation.

The initial rules regarding hats became a Keystone Kops situation. Since about 50% of the male student population of Cascade Jr. High wore hats to class, the first directive from the administration said students could wear hats between classes, but must remove them during class time. When the bell rang to dismiss class, hat wearers could put them on to wear while traveling between periods. Upon reaching the next class, the hat wearers had to doff their chapeaus, and wait for the bell to again put their headgear on for the five minutes that was the passing time. It soon became obvious this system did not work. Students forgot to remove their hats upon reaching their class, and there was no end of conflicts between teachers, administrators, and students about the rules regarding hats in school. Since there could be some legitimate reasons for wearing headgear; students who had undergone chemotherapy, male Jewish students observing religious requirements, Sikh pupils whose traditions required the covering of their hair, and others who had a legitimate claim to cover their head, this turned into a ridiculous example of how a small group of bureaucrats can create a huge problem out of virtually nothing by micromanaging. Some people advocated a total ban on hats, while others wanted to further tweak the existing rules.

In response to the confusion about hats and their place in the school and classroom, I wrote and distributed the following, which started at Cascade, but soon found its way to most other schools in the district:

To: District Employees
From: Dress Code Committee
Re: Hats

There has been a great deal of confusion about the issue of hat wearing at school, and how that complies with, or conflicts with state or district policy. The specific codicil dealing with this issue may be found in Subsection 4, Section 3 (R.C.W. 27-38-27.58). The section reads in part:

". . . any student activity controlled by educational need or directives which conflict with apparel considered seditious

or in anywise unusual to the a priori operation of any of the common schools of the state of Washington or of its immediate

environs, shall be at the discretion of any legitimately elected board or its equivalent incumbent. The needs of the school

community as a whole shall be a prime consideration in the implementation of specific controlling factors which may or

may not be present at the time of its adoption. Nothing herein shall be construed to disparage the legitimate psychomotor

concerns of individual cases on a specific ex post facto basis . . . "

It is clear this passage has given legitimate credence to the district guidelines regarding hats. But it also opens a series of loopholes through which some nefarious miscreant(s) might wriggle.

Any student desiring an exemption to the no-hat rule must fit within the following guidelines:

EXCEPTIONS:

1. Any student wearing a **burnoose** because of socio-religious factors must be able to converse in fluent Farsi, or be able to trace Selucid caliphs' (any three) lineage through at least five generations.

2. Any student sporting a **yarmulke** must demonstrate his knowledge of the Pentateuch and the significance of a Seder tree.

3. Any **miter** worn to school should be clean and without sin.

4. A **fez**-wearing youngster must be able to recite the inaugural address of Kemal Ataturk (1918).

5. Any **turbaned** fellow (or fellah) must be able to quote chapter and verse from the **Bhagavad-Gita.** Note: Any attempt to substitute an intimate knowledge of the cadences of the **Kama-Sutra** instead will be met with immediate rejection.

6. Any **wimple**-wearing student must demonstrate an expert's knowledge of the rules of chivalrous conduct, and be able, on demand, to deliver a brief biographical account of the life of Eleanor of Aquitaine.

7. A student wearing a **tam o' shanter** should be required to recite at least two verses of "Willie Brewed a Peck o' Mout," or "Scots, Wha Hae," along with a brief narrative of the life of Bonnie Bobby Burns.

8. Anyone sporting a **pith helmet** must demonstrate knowledge of the concepts of Pax Britannica, and be able, without notes, to recite at least two verses of "Gunga Din," "Tommy," or "The Light That Failed."

9. Any **shako**-wearing student shall immediately be brought to attention, and be required to demonstrate the entire Military

Manual of Arms, as well as recite provisions of the GENEVA CONVENTION'S rules of war.

10. Any student wearing a **bicorne** must compare and contrast the Code Napoleon with either the Laws of Hammurabi, or at the very least, the Justinian Code. Note: any **bicorne** sans cockade should not be allowed under any circumstances.

11. Since **snoods** are on the cutting edge of hatdom, individual discretion with wide latitude should be observed. Note should be taken as to color, shape and size before a definitive decision regarding de-**snooding** a particular individual is made.

12. Any student wearing a **templette** should be able to discuss the economic policies of Lorenzo de Medici, and to compare and contrast the financial dealings of the Italian Renaissance bankers with the Fuggers of Germany.

13. Any student wearing a Cardinal's **biretta** or a priest's **zucchetto** should be able to carry on a discourse defending the Ptolemaic view of the solar system, and effectively rebut the Copernican challenge to established order.

14. Any student flaunting a **mortarboard** anytime other than during an officially sanctioned school district ceremony must be able to sing at least two verses of Pomp and Circumstance a capella, in Latin. An exception may be granted to any pupil able to prove a genetic link to Mortimer Adler, James B. Conant, or John Dewey.

The above list is by no means complete. Every district employee should remain alert to the possibilities of student noncompliance with legitimate rules. It is important that we continue to remember the maxim:

"FIRST, HATS, TOMORROW, THE WORLD!"

I got several reactions from a number of people, most of whom realized how ridiculous it was to micromanage hat wearing. Allow it, or ban it. The attempt to let some exceptions through the cracks merely encouraged students to push the hat rules (actually, good for them!) My favorite response was from one of my most respected colleagues, John Sutherland, who also shares the belief that large monolithic entities, such as some educational edifices need to be poked occasionally.

John's response to the Dress Code, hat division:
Dear Don:

Hats off to you for your article on the dress code. It may be old hat to some, but your explication of the mad hatter statute capped your long career as a writer—another feather in your cap, as it were.

The student protest (against hat rules) no doubt demonstrated to the kids that the brass hats meant business. No talking through their hats this time. When the youngsters get a bee in their bonnets again, they should keep it under their hats because if they set their caps and invite capitulation, they'll just end up going hat-in-hand to beg forgiveness. Eating one's hat is no fun. Neither is having your "rights" knocked into a cocked hat.

Again, the article is your crowning glory. If we ever elect a president of satire, your hat will be in the ring, so to speak.

Uncaptiously,
John Sutherland

Retirement Musings

© 2018, JoAnn Lakin Jackson

When I went to my retirement party, I stood there enjoying seeing so many former students, parents, and old friends that I have made over the years as well as many colleagues. My children had a hand in the festivities as well, featuring a bagpiper to help set the tone for the event.

I thought about when I first started teaching, back when the school district I applied to had just ended a battle with a much larger, more influential district. They were in a small town, and were left with one building (built in 1907) and would be able to conduct school for grades K through 8 with a total population of 60.

I had graduated on Sunday, applied on Wednesday, hired on Friday. Many thought the school would not last, maybe not even a year. I figured I did not have anything to lose as there were not many jobs available at that time.

I was given a room. I went in and was immediately over-whelmed. It was empty, I mean really empty---no desks, no nothing. I loved the wooden floors and large windows that came down to my waist but rose perhaps ten feet. The small squares of each pane gave it a homey appearance.

On the other side of the room there was one door and a wall of blackboard sections which could be pulled up to reveal places for coats, boots, or any other storage. The back of the room had a counter over cupboards across the whole space. The room was huge, one could put perhaps sixty desks in it. I remember the sound seemed so accented as I walked in that empty space.

Now I have a room that is fully carpeted except for one small area. They are not as comfortable to stand on all day as those old wooden ones were. It is quiet and dark as it has smaller windows which have venetian blinds built in. Those tall windows

I began with had no curtains at all. I remember wondering how cold the room might be in the winter. My room now has a thermostat that I am free to adjust.

We have just renovated this building; all is new. As part of the updating, they would not even let me keep my wonderful heavy wooden chairs, replacing them with color-coordinated plastic ones (how I hate them). I wonder how long they will last. I had my others for thirty-seven years and they were not new then. I even had three sizes to accommodate different size children. When you sat on them they were warm and comfortable. These new plastic ones are cold and uninviting as well as less sturdy--- but they look nice.

Going back to the very beginning, I was thirty-eight and had four children so I had some idea of what I needed to teach a class, but there was nothing in this big silent space. I did not even know at that point how many children I would have or how many of each grade I should plan on. I only knew I was to have Kindergarten, First and Second Grade.

I went to the Principal/Superintendent for direction. He said, "Go around the building, if you see something you want, take it or ask the custodian to take it to your room." I found most of what I wanted in the library. Some round tables and stools, a book display case, and in the art room I found some wonderful storage cabinets on wheels that had wonderful vinyl tops. I still use them   now. When they took the building down last year to renovate I 'surplused' some and took them home— they were going to be thrown away (actually sent to the dump). The reason? They would not fit in with the planned décor.

Today I have one grade to teach and have had for most of my years here, but back then, at the beginning, I was going to have three.

There were no supplies, no toys for kindergarten children. The superintendent told me to go to the school they had lost to the other district and ask for what I needed from one of their rooms.

They laughed at me and told me to go away. I returned to my school to report what I was told.

He took my list and returned with about five items.

I think about my room now. I have the most expanded group of blocks a teacher could have. I am so pleased with what I have acquired over the years. Frank Lloyd Wright said that he felt his beginning in architecture came from the wonderful set of blocks his mother gave him when he was three-years-old. I gave my son a set of blocks and added to them when he was three-years-old. They were well used for a great many years. I even caught one of my daughter's nineteen-year old boy friends building with them once..

Anyway, back then I had no blocks. I made a deal with my son to borrow them for my classroom for September until Christmas. So my kindergarteners then had blocks.

Now I even have unusual pieces I have acquired from a woodworker friend of mine. I have at least four cabinets full, plus a few large boxes with unusual pieces. Hopefully my replacement will appreciate what she is receiving.

There was a teacher who was planning to be there once school had started my first year but in the deal that was made, all teachers who worked there were given a guarantee of one year working in their district. Only two stayed, the rest left, thus my job was available. She had ordered a beginning-to-read program for kindergarteners. As it turned out, it was an excellent program which I used and expanded on. Even now I use its basic concepts, with a great deal of success.

But I had nothing for first or second grade students. No guidelines, just, NOTHING. I went to the library and managed to find an old book that gave the expectations for each grade level—written thirty years before, but at least I had something to work with.

Recently we wrote up new expectations for our district, I had a hand in the new guidelines. How times have changed.

Now I can plan at the end of the year for what I will need

next year and order it, then, unless there turns out to be some major budget restriction, my supplies for next year will come. This year I tried to order what I think another teacher would like to have.

But that first year, I had to find old textbooks and books from the library (but not our library; they were for older children) for the children to read, anything else we did, I had to make up or present on my own.

The Superintendent is here to present me with an award for all my years of service. He is new; he doesn't really know me, but that's okay, everyone else here knows me, and I know them.

How wonderful to see so many old familiar faces. One of my first students is here, she was one of my first First Grade students. She works in the main office for the school district now.

Another of my first students is here. When I began I had ten students. The other grade school teacher had third, fourth and fifth grade, for a total of nineteen students. She immediately went to the Superintendent and complained that she had so many more than I did. She wanted to give me the third grade for half of the day each day. I replied I would rather take them for the whole day. Since three of them were special education students she agreed in one hot minute.

I had figured they were working at a first grade level so it was a better fit. Jerry was one of those students. Towering over everyone else in my class, he was a third grade student but he had been held back twice. Even so, he functioned at a first grade level. Here he was now, tall, happy, engaged, working---proudly pointing to his second new truck. He had come to see me to show off his first shiny new red truck after earning enough money to buy it when he graduated from high school. Now he is a well-thought -of person in his community, perhaps not with 'the sharpest pencil', but functioning well and very content. This warms my heart to think of how far he has come.

He was one of my challenges then. His idea of working on a paper was to lie on the seat and place his paper on the floor to work on it. His writing was non-legible. (All of my students learn to write legibly, actually neatly now.) I decided to teach him cursive. I modeled it on the board using my left hand. Sitting up in his chair, he learned to write.

I have never had a student like Jerry since. Now I have a student who cannot speak English and his father comes into class three days a week to interpret for him.

That second week of school when I started, suddenly, after a school board meeting, the Superintendent was fired! It turned out he was found to be a person who was working for the will of the district we had just lost our other schools to. He was there to make it fail. They found him out, they fired him.

Then they hired a former math teacher who had a fire in his belly. Totally unlike the quiet man who runs our district now. Al saw this as a group of young people isolated from real society and he was going to teach them and teach them what there was out there in the world.

Now I rarely see the Superintendent; I saw Al all the time. He said that I should always remember that what I did should have a lasting memory on my students. Have I done that? Is that why there are so many people here today? The gym if full, so many faces to remember and now I remember so many things we did at that first school before we consolidated with this district.

This year being the last, I decided to do exactly whatever I wanted, but without a lot of announcement ahead of time. The other teachers don't like to put on plays. I do. I did.

But back to Jerry. He and his friend, also a third grader, would skip school frequently. They would go fishing. I would notify Al, he would call the town policeman who guessed where they were, go find them and bring them to class. This happened numerous times.

Nothing like this would happen now. But we were successful. I decided on a plan. I gave these two boys a set amount of work each day. They were to finish it before they went home. I told their parents they would not be home till it was done. I let my caretakers for my children know I would be home late for a while. The boys procrastinated, did not finish their work, expecting to run out with the others. I did not let them. I stayed, they worked, saw I meant it, so they finished. This happened three days and never again. Nor did they ever skip school again. I am not sure I would be allowed to do this today, but it was very effective and had a lifelong effect on them.

The other boy has moved away, but Jerry still lives in the same community and everyone loves him and his hard-working ethic.

This year has been full of joy. My students have all been successful; they had so much fun working hard. They put on several plays and the final art project turned out to be a forty-five-foot mural, three feet high, of wild horses racing across the wall on a black background. Each horse had been painted by splattering or throwing paint onto a form of a horse in a color of their choice which was butcher paper, then cut out to join the racing herd.

Many people came to see it and photograph it, including a newspaper. What made it so spectacular was it was a new, pristine wall. After our class play, children took their parents to the hall to show off their special horse. Fifty horses racing in this manner gives me a great deal of pleasure knowing that two sessions of kindergarteners could create such an effect.

During those first two years, I did not have the supplies or the space for such a project.

Now, the principal expects a weird and extensive list of supplies on my request form for next years' needs. Back then I had no form for any request.

But when the new Principal/Superintendent, Al Carpenter, came, he began to ask me what I might need. I just knew it should not be very much. Now I have a budget and can ask for what I want as long as it is within my limits.

This year I smile when I think of the field trips we have taken. They have been meaningful, informative, and fun. Back then, Al made them a challenge. We did not plan them; he did, with no consideration for time or our personal requirements for our own families. We were expected to give 110% or more—at any time. Now the union would make sure we were within certain limits and hours.

One of the trips our Principal, Al, decided on was a ski trip for the whole school. A kindergarten child's mother asked if I felt it was one she should keep her child home from. He was a very young child. I said 'yes'. Al heard about it and called me in his office and challenged my judgement. I stood my ground (with shaking boots). The child went with us. On the way home Al sat with the child. He pooped his pants. Al did not say anything more to me about what I had told the parent.

On another occasion, Al bought a boat, he named it The Educator. We were to be at school at 6 a.m. and expect not to return before 6 p.m. When I told him of my children's complex schedule, he said, "no fear, my secretary will do it for you." She did. I picked my kids up at her house at 7 that evening at a church social she needed to attend.

Now, our trips are carefully coordinated with the other schools needs for the buses. Fun but not nearly as challenging as Al's sudden choices.

Here we are, in a nice, new, updated building. All warm and cozy, but almost no storage. I think back to that big old building I started in. I think back to the day, Al came to get me. He showed me one of the many closets you could climb up into the attic in, then we scurried down the hall to other end of the building and waited in silence. Suddenly, before us appeared an 8th grade student out of the closet. He had run across the attic. He had been using this as a way to leave the room and leave school. He denied vehemently that he had done it. But we just followed him and saw him come out of the closet. He believed his own lies.

Then there was the spring day the skunks had a fight in the

basement. This is the most awful, truly sickening smell possible! We had to close the school for several days until specialists could come minimize the odor. It did not totally go away for a long time. No such thing can happen here—we don't have a basement.

I am so happy to look back at the beginning, the parents I made friends with, the children I have seen grow and become wonderful, interesting adults. I would like to think both then and now, I sparked an interest in learning, questioning, and love of literature and music as well as the need for exercise and desire to try new things. I loved my life then and I love it now.

Current 2018
Plateau Area Writers Association
Officers

President
JoAnn Lakin Jackson
Thru 2019

Vice President
Kenneth S. Lapham
Thru 2018

Finance Officer
Marilyn R. Glasscock
Thru 2018

Recorder
Jana Nielsen
Thru 2019

Public Relations
Web Master
Larry Krack
Thru 2019

Publications Editor
Paul T. Jackson
Thru 2018

Editorial Board
Don Hagen
Larry Krackle

A 501(c)3 organization
An EBSCOhost Publication
Member, South King County
Cultural Coalition

Current 2018 Critique Groups

NEW:

Inspired Writers for Children? Meets monthly at members' homes. Present contact: Jana Neilson 253-561-2120 - whitecloud.graphics@gmail.com

NEW:

Bonney Lake Critique group: Meets at the Bonney Lake Senior Center Tuesdays, 1pm. Contact Larry Krack, Larrykrackle@gmail.com or 253-222-9705. two positions are open.

Baker Street Writers Meets at the Black Diamond Bakery. 1st & 3rd Wednesdays, 10:00 a.m. Currently filled; but possible opening. Contact info: Ardi Butler 425-432-4154 ardibutler@comcast.net

Green River Writers Guild: Monthly meetings rotate in members' homes. Filled. Contact: Richard Brugger 253-833-9181 RKBrugger@comcast.net

Writer's Reading Group: Meets the 5th Friday of the month (Quarterly) 10:00-noon, with lunch. Meet at High Point Village. Any member wanting to read their work is invited. Contact info: Laura Curnan 360 825-7780 jlcurnan@msn.com.

ISBN 978-0-916262-77-8

9 780916 262778

Made in the USA
San Bernardino, CA
23 November 2018